Let the dream of a safer tomorrow become a reality as we give our children
the tools to make it possible.

Manufactured in the United States of America 10 9 8 7 6 5 4 3

Library of Congress Catalog Card Number: 96-71670

Rafael, Janis Paula: Playing It Safe With Mr. See-More Safety — Let's Rap and Rhyme — Summary: Poems that teach children how to be careful in everyday life by encouraging awareness and the development of critical thinking skills.

First Edition

ISBN: 978-0-9655604-0-5 (softcover)
ISBN: 978-0-9655604-3-6 (e-book-EPUB)
ISBN: 978-0-9655604-4-3 (PDF)

See-More Safety Productions, an imprint of Safeworld Publishing Company.

In memory of my father, Mr. Seymour (See-More) Lessans
(September 29, 1918-January 29, 1991)
who was my mentor and my inspiration.
May you all join me in the vital mission of creating
a safe world for our children,
and for all future generations to come.

A MOTHER'S PRAYER

As our children go out in the world each day,
may they be safe in God's keeping and out of harm's way.
As I give them my heart and all of my love,
I ask for the wisdom that comes from above.
May they learn all the things they will need to know,
to help keep them safe as they continue to grow.
To help them become all they were meant to be...
this is what I beseech of thee.
To give them the knowledge, to show them the way,
to help keep them safe while they grow and they play.
This is what I ask for and all that I pray...
to keep our children safe as they begin each new day

TABLE OF CONTENTS

A MESSAGE TO PARENTS AND TEACHERS

Playing It Safe With Mr. See-More Safety™ — Let's Rap and Rhyme — is the first of a series dedicated to teaching children how to be safety conscious as they leave their parents' protective arms and begin taking their first steps toward independence. The poetic style offers children a way to remember important concepts through the use of repetition and rhyme. As children listen to the rhymes, they will begin to refer to them in their everyday lives. The animated character, Mr. See-More Safety, was created to be a friend to children by encouraging them to make safer choices. Although entertainment is important so children will not lose interest, the objective is for these safety messages to become firmly established. These rhymes are filled with vital information which parents often assume children know, but in actuality, may not. By receiving valuable safety instruction at an early age, children will have a chance to develop sound habits that will last a lifetime.

Playing It Safe With Mr. See-More Safety was written for children of all ages. Parents can enjoy the illustrations with very young children and at the same time help them interpret the significance of what is being portrayed. As children begin to read, the words will reinforce the illustrations which they are already familiar with. By observing and carefully discussing each scene with a parent or teacher, children will be helped to identify the kind of situations that could lead to an accident. Consequently, they will be in a much better position to know what to do should they ever be faced with a real life situation.

As children enter each new stage of development, they will have a better understanding of "cause and effect" and the connection between a person's actions and the consequences that could follow. Allowing children to role play scenarios that contain hidden dangers will help them see how easy it is for just the "right" circumstances to lead to disaster. This interactive method fosters active participation in the learning process, thus making the information easier for children to understand and apply. Moreover, sharing the rhymes with older children will open up an avenue for discussion which could prove to be extremely beneficial. By using this book as a springboard for ongoing dialogue, children will have an opportunity to clarify important safety issues in relation to their own lives.

1

It is our hope that Mr. See-More Safety will become a role model so children will have a strong desire to emulate him. His positive influence will help them resist negative peer pressure to act in an irresponsible or dangerous manner. Mr. See-More Safety's goal is to teach children how to identify serious risks in their environment and find ways to eliminate them where they have the ability to do so. He approaches the topic of safety in a gentle fashion, but due to the seriousness of the subject matter the illustrations, as well as the text, must send a powerful message and cannot be watered-down. Some of the terminology will be new and may need to be defined, but the words will become automatic as the vocabulary is repeated and understood in context. A glossary has been provided for this purpose. To help children feel the rhythm and express the poems in tempo, the symbol (...) indicating where to pause is used throughout the book.

Although it is true that the earlier children develop sound safety habits, the better...it is never too late. The issue of safety must continue to be our first priority because our children are our most precious gifts. We hope Mr. See-More Safety becomes a welcome partner in the effort to help children think critically and perceptively, thereby preventing the conditions that so often lead to tragedy. We must make every effort to give our children the tools that will help them to be as safe as possible. So without further ado, let us begin working together to achieve this most important mission!

THE BOUNCING BALL

HEY GUYS AND GALS, I hope you all...can...see...
that acting on impulse is as DANGEROUS as can be.
You gotta HOLD...BACK before you go for that ball...
If it goes in the street...you gotta check...THAT'S ALL!
But ALWAYS...REMEMBER...that just before you go,
you gotta LOOK...BOTH...WAYS...then
GO SAFELY GO!
You need to <u>ALWAYS</u>...<u>REMEMBER</u>...that just before
you go, you gotta LOOK...BOTH...WAYS...then
<u>GO SAFELY GO</u>!

URGENT MESSAGE FROM MR. SEE-MORE SAFETY:

Running into the street without checking first is extremely dangerous and is called "acting on impulse." In order to prevent yourself from acting impulsively, it is important to notice the feeling that occurs right before you make a sudden move. As you become familiar with this feeling, you will be able to stop yourself in just enough time to carefully check for danger first. Training yourself <u>never</u> to act on impulse — especially in a situation that could be dangerous such as playing near the street — may help prevent a serious accident. This is a skill that requires practice in a safe environment. Once you acquire it, it will help to protect you in a real life situation. Don't ever put yourself in a dangerous position in order to test your ability!

BUCKLE UP KIDS

When you're out for a ride…in the car you will see
that being buckled up for safety is the WAY to be.
You must be SURE…each…time…that you get in the car…
to lock your seat belt in, and you'll be safer BY FAR.
For you NEVER know when there will come a time…
that your SAFETY BELT will be your only lifeline!
So before you get in…remember CLICK the belt in…
and you will BEAT THE ODDS…IN THE END
YOU WILL WIN!

URGENT MESSAGE FROM MR. SEE-MORE SAFETY:

KIDS, don't wait for the driver to tell you to wear your seat belt. She may forget to remind you, and this is an important decision you need to make for yourself. Make it a habit to put your seat belt on the minute you get in the car. It only takes a few seconds, but it could save your life! The strap should fit securely around your hips. If it feels loose, or there is a space between your hips and the belt, make sure to tighten it or get an adult to help you. The shoulder strap should be adjusted so it crosses your chest. It should not rub against your neck. You may need a booster seat to make the seat belt fit properly. Remember, it is up to YOU to put your seat belt on. It cannot protect you unless you use it, so BE A "SAFE SMART KID" AND CLICK THE BELT IN!

COME AND GET IT!

When you're sitting down at mealtime…
and you're HUNGRY as a bear…
this is just the time you need to eat
with TENDER LOVING CARE.
As you chew your food too quickly, it
could go down the wrong way…
and you'd begin to CHOKE and
not be able a word to say.
Sitting down at mealtime REALLY
should be nice and slow…

for there's danger when you rush...
and you're ALWAYS ON THE GO.
One bite could slip down the wrong
way, and YOU'D begin to CHOKE...
as you take too big a swallow and it
gets caught IN YOUR THROAT.
So chew you're food CAREFULLY when
you're HUNGRY AS A BEAR...
and treat the SPECIAL TIME you eat with
TENDER LOVING CARE!

URGENT MESSAGE FROM MR. SEE-MORE SAFETY:

BOYS AND GIRLS, please remember that talking while eating may cause
choking. If you are in a hurry to finish, it will add to the risk, especially if you
are not taking the time to carefully chew and swallow. If you begin to choke,
let someone know by pointing to your throat. If no one is there, learn the
Heimlich maneuver so you will be able to help yourself. KIDS, also be aware
that pulling on pen tops, or trying to yank lollipops from their sticks can result
in choking. Keep foreign objects away from your mouth. DO <u>NOT</u> USE your
teeth to try to open or pry something apart, especially if the object is small
enough to swallow. If you should happen to pull it loose, the force could
propel the object to the back of your throat, causing you to choke! With a
little precaution, you will avoid the risk of choking because you took the
<u>extra</u> time and care!

COME HERE LITTLE DOGGY

When you see a strange animal that you REALLY
do not know,
Be CAREFUL WHILE petting it; it could BITE your
finger or toe.
Always approach this animal...VERY VERY SLOW...
and talk to it gently as you SOFTLY say hello.
Don't EVER take a chance and put your face
too close to his...
he could suddenly become STARTLED...and BITE

9

you in a whiz.
You must look for little signs that he may NOT
want you around...
a snarl or a tail tucked in, or even an angry sound
(Grrrrrrrrrr)!
So please be VERY CAREFUL when an animal
walks up to YOU...
and you'll prevent a NASTY bite, cause you knew
JUST WHAT TO DO!

URGENT MESSAGE FROM MR. SEE-MORE SAFETY:

<u>NEVER</u>, approach a wild or stray animal even if it looks friendly, wild animals are known to carry rabies, and if they bite you, you may need to go through a series of shots to make sure rabies does not pass on to you. Animals that you do not know can be unpredictable, so remember to <u>ALWAYS</u> keep your distance to avoid getting bitten.

DON'T LIGHT A FIRE

Don't EVER play with matches if you HAPPEN...to see...
them lying on the FLOOR...by a BED...or
a TREE.
Tell your MOM...or your DAD...EXACTLY what you see...
but remember NEVER touch them, don't forget...
LET THEM BE!
MATCHES are not playthings, they can BURN...so you see...
you should NEVER play with matches, DO NOT TOUCH...
LET THEM BE!

URGENT MESSAGE FROM MR. SEE-MORE SAFETY:

If you see kids playing with matches, go tell an adult. Your quick action may prevent a tragedy. Sometimes it is more important to do what is right than it is to be popular. In the long run you will be respected for your courage, even though your friends may be angry at you at first and may even call you a tattletale. Remember, matches can be dangerous. Don't allow your dreams — or the dreams of others — to go up in smoke! Did you know that cigarette lighters can be just as dangerous as matches? After flicking the lighter, a very large flame might suddenly burst forth which could allow your clothes or hair to catch on fire. Be on the lookout for lighters that are disguised as something else. If you happen to see a lighter lying on the ground...DON'T TOUCH IT! If a very young child is playing with a lighter, take it away immediately and give it to an adult!

ENGINE ENGINE NUMBER 7

CHUG A CHUG A, CHUG A CHUG A,
CHUG A CHUG A, CHOO CHOO...CHOO CHOO
When a train is coming down the railroad track...you should
<u>NEVER</u> play close...you should stay WAY BACK.
This is <u>NOT</u> the right time to EVER try and see...how fast
your bike can go…or how quick your legs can be.
You need to STOP, LOOK, AND LISTEN...don't forget
to WAIT…when the train whistle blows at the crossing gate.
You need to STOP, LOOK, AND LISTEN...

don't forget to <u>WAIT</u>...when the train
whistle blows at the crossing gate.
CHUG A CHUG A, CHUG A CHUG A, CHUG A CHUGA,
CHUG A CHUG A, CHOO CHOO...CHOO CHOO

URGENT MESSAGE FROM MR. SEE-MORE SAFETY

If you see a train coming, DO NOT ATTEMPT TO CROSS! It is very easy to misjudge the speed of an oncoming train, so don't even try! Remember, you are becoming "safe smart kids" by learning to make the safest choice. It isn't worth it to try and prove how fast you can go just to get home a few seconds earlier. Sooner or later you could lose. If you live near railroad tracks, DO NOT play there! Someone may try and dare you to play dangerous games such as running across to beat the train. This could end up with tragic consequences. So learn to be the CONDUCTOR OF YOUR LIFE, and <u>CHOOSE</u> to stay away from the tracks!

FROM HEAD TO TOE

When you're with your friends...on the playground at school...
PLAY IT SAFE, KIDS...PLAY IT COOL.
Don't EVER wear jewelry or strings that are loose...AROUND
YOUR NECK, they could become a noose!
Tell your MOM to take...the drawstrings from your hood...replace
them with snaps, for SAFETY'S SAKE YOU <u>SHOULD</u>.
And when your shoestrings ARE JUST WAITING to get caught...
bend down and tie them tight as you have been TAUGHT!
If you take these precautions...BEFORE you go to play, you'll be
helping TO STAY...<u>OUT</u> OF HARM'S WAY!

15

URGENT MESSAGE FROM MR. SEE-MORE SAFETY:

Long necklaces, scarves, or ornaments that dangle or have beads or toggles attached should be worn with extreme caution. They could suddenly get caught on a swing or sliding board, causing strangulation. The straps on a backpack could be very dangerous if they get caught on a bus handrail or a car door as you are exiting. Untied shoestrings can be a serious hazard if they get stuck in the space between the steps of a moving escalator, or tangled in the spokes of a bicycle wheel. Make sure you have your shoelaces tied so they don't come loose. You can make the decision to "play it safe" by becoming extremely careful when wearing clothing, jewelry, or accessories that hang or have loops. For example, you may choose to wear hanging jewelry on special occasions or during safe activities. By making small changes beforehand, you can eliminate this danger!

GAMES KIDS PLAY

KIDS, LISTEN UP, I just want you to know...that cars can be
DANGEROUS...wherever you go.
You should <u>NEVER</u> play in driveways where a driver may not
see...you sitting playing jacks or cards, or a game of Monopoly.
The driver could back up...and not EVER be aware...that you're
playing in the driveway without EVEN A CARE!
So <u>NEVER</u> play in driveways where a driver may not see...you
sitting playing kids games, there could be a TRAGEDY!
You've got to <u>ALWAYS</u> PLAY IT SAFE...play where CARS

CANNOT DRIVE!
By being SAFE SMART KIDS, you'll keep each other ALIVE!

URGENT MESSAGE FROM MR. SEE-MORE SAFETY:

CARS AND KIDS can be a dangerous mix. Always double-check when you are playing outside to make sure there is <u>NO</u> chance for a car to back up and accidentally hit you. This could easily occur in a parking lot, cul-de-sac, alley, or on a quiet street. You may have received a false impression that these quiet areas are safe to play, but they could be just as dangerous as driveways if the driver is unable to see you in his rear-view mirror. This is an easy setup for an accident since the driver may have no idea you are playing directly behind his vehicle. Remember, if you choose to play where cars are <u>not</u> allowed, there will be NO POSSIBILITY for a car to suddenly back up and hit you. AND YOU WILL BE ONE "SAFE SMART KID!"

GIVE IT TO ME, I HAD IT FIRST

If you're EVER struggling in a TUG OF WAR...
it's easy to get hurt, something you CANNOT ignore.
As you compete for the "prize," and you think you've got it made,
there are safety rules to follow...which MUST BE OBEYED.
You should NEVER pull on objects that are sharp, such as sticks,
that could BOOMERANG...causing some serious nicks.
And if the object you are pulling SNAPS <u>BACK</u> toward your eye,
that's the place it will go...causing YOU to cry!
This game could end up hurting someone SERIOUSLY...when
you're pulling on an object...AS HARD AS CAN BE!

19

Cause when you're in a TUG OF WAR sharp objects could fly,
and come back hitting you................BULLS EYE!!

URGENT MESSAGE FROM MR. SEE-MORE SAFETY:

As you can see, tug of war needs to be played with caution. Never pull on an object that is sharp — or can stretch — and suddenly snap back at you with a lot of force. If the other person decides to let go, you could fall backwards, possibly hitting your head on a sharp object. Another related danger is when you push on something too hard and the force causes it to break. If it happens to be a glass bottle or glass door, it could be extremely dangerous. If the object won't open, even though you are applying a lot of pressure, it is time to let go. You shouldn't have to use all of your strength to open something. If it is a fragile object it could shatter, causing someone to get seriously injured.

GO FOR THE GOLD

Whatever sport you may decide to play this year...please
make sure to wear <u>ALL</u> of your protective gear.
You may play Little League...Football...or Hockey, too...
whatever sport you choose, your gear will help protect you.
It was made to keep you SAFE...if you...should...fall...
or you happen to get hit...by a SPEEDING BALL.
If a skater would slip and land directly on his knee, pads
would help prevent stitches...AMAZINGLY!
A player could...slide...and hit his head on the ground...
without a helmet on, his head would REALLY pound!

21

So why not wear your MOUTH GUARDS, PADS AND
HELMETS this year...and be SAFE...thanks to <u>ALL</u> OF
YOUR PROTECTIVE GEAR!

URGENT MESSAGE FROM MR. SEE-MORE SAFETY:

BOYS AND GIRLS, it's very easy to forget to put on your safety gear when you're in a hurry to play sports or ride bikes, but this important step will help to keep you safe. Your safety equipment will protect you from unexpected falls, blows to the head, or damage to your eyes. In fact, there is no better way to protect yourself against serious sports injuries than to wear your helmets, pads, and goggles. So get into the habit of reaching for your safety gear EVERY TIME you go out to play. Learn to be "SAFE SMART KIDS" and GO FOR THE GOLD!

HERE I COME, MOM

If your mom should call you from across the street...
or you see a friend...who you've been waiting to meet...
you must <u>ALWAYS</u> remember to HES-I-TATE...before
crossing the street...or it could be TOO LATE!
You need to STOP, LOOK and LISTEN...for a few
seconds...<u>WAIT!</u>...DO NOT begin to cross the street
until you HES-I-TATE!
Remember: STOP, LOOK, AND LISTEN...for a few
seconds...<u>WAIT!</u>   DON'T EVER start to cross the
street until you...<u>HES-I-TATE</u>!!

URGENT MESSAGE FROM MR. SEE-MORE SAFETY:

It is important to remember that anytime you "act on impulse," you could be at risk for an accident, especially if you are distracted by someone calling to you from across the street. You could easily forget to look both ways first. This is why it is necessary for you for you to identify the feeling that occurs right before you make an impulsive move. You will then be able to stop yourself in enough time to check for oncoming traffic first, before darting into the street without thinking. Learning to hesitate for these critical few seconds, could one day save your life, and the reason it is worth repeating. Once you step into the street, any hesitation at all could be dangerous, so you should always check <u>before</u> you begin crossing. If the light suddenly turns green before you have reached the other side, check to make sure the cars see you as you are making your way across.

HIDING PLACES

If you happen to be walking...down the street...and you
see an empty fridge that REALLY looks neat...you
should NEVER climb in...to take a peek...even if it's a
perfect place for "hide-and-go-seek."
You may get locked inside...and without any keys, you
could get TRAPPED...and soon...NOT BE ABLE
TO BREATHE!
So the message here...is very simple and clear...if you're
NOT sure of the danger, you should <u>NEVER</u> GO NEAR!

URGENT MESSAGE FROM MR. SEE-MORE SAFETY:

Kids, DON'T hide in narrow or cramped places because you could get stuck and not be able to pull yourself back out. NEVER climb into an open space head first. Your body could get stuck and act like a plug. With no one there to pull you out, you could suffocate. DO NOT climb into anything that has doors that could lock behind you like refrigerators and trunks of cars. BEWARE of drainage ditches, wells, and sewers. These may look like fun places to hide but could end up just the opposite if the unexpected happens. Be sure to stay away from construction sites that could suddenly cave in. Homemade forts made out of loose rocks, bricks, sand (either wet or dry), or deep snow could collapse with you underneath. Another danger is hiding in a pile of leaves, especially if it is beside a curb. Someone may begin parking and ride over the leaves with you inside. Don't EVER hide in trash bags for the same reason. So when you're playing hide-and-go seek, always remember: IF YOU'RE NOT SURE OF THE DANGER, you should NEVER GO NEAR!

HIGHER AND HIGHER WE GO

When you're playing in your backyard...climbing trees...
it may look so EASY; it may look like a breeze.
But DON'T BE FOOLED by WHAT YOU SEE...cause
the risk is serious; I know you'll agree.
There is ALWAYS the chance that YOU MAY FALL
from a big, old tree standing HIGH, standing TALL.
A branch could SNAP as you turn around, and you'd
come tumbling right down...DOWN TO THE GROUND!
A BIGGER danger as you climb even higher, is the SHOCK

you could get from an electrical wire.
And as you're climbing back down from those big old trees,
you could come face-to-face with a SWARM OF BEES!
So when you're making a choice RIGHT...FROM...THE...
START, CHOOSE <u>NOT</u> TO CLIMB TREES, and
PLAY IT SMART!

URGENT MESSAGE FROM MR. SEE-MORE SAFETY:

Outside electrical wires are not insulated and they contain a high voltage of electricity. You could get electrocuted if you touch them. They are also called overhead lines, or high tension wires. If an overhead line is close to a tree, DO NOT GO NEAR THAT TREE! If you still decide to climb trees, BE A SMART CLIMBER. Don't go very high, so even if you fall you won't get hurt. Check to make sure the branches are strong enough to hold your weight. You can make the choice to "PLAY IT SMART."

HOME SWEET HOME

When you're HOME...from...school...at the end of the
day...make sure to put ALL of your belongings away.
There may be COATS...and NOTEBOOKS...and TOYS
on the floor...and the stairway going up...may be filled
even more.
A person could FALL...as he walks into the room because
papers, books, and toys...are EVERYWHERE strewn.
This is NOT...the way...for your HOME to be...it should
be <u>SAFE</u>...<u>FROM</u>...<u>FALLS</u>, and it's easy, YOU'LL SEE.

You just put your things away...at the end of the day...
and your home will be much safer, IT WILL BE
A OKAY!

URGENT MESSAGE FROM MR. SEE-MORE SAFETY:

Don't be CARELESS with your belongings! BE <u>CAREFUL</u>! Get into the habit of putting your things in a special place. This will help prevent someone from tripping. Toys, costs, and books do not belong on the floor — or steps — where a person may not see them. Becoming better organized will help you keep your home free of clutter. By putting your belongings away each time you use them, you will be eliminating the risk of someone falling and getting injured. This will prevent an accident <u>before</u> it has a chance to occur. Always make sure to clean up spills right away so no one slips. Your parents will be so proud of you for keeping everyone safe!

I CAN'T REACH IT

Don't EVER climb on furniture...to reach for your
favorite toy. It could suddenly fall right down on
you...and this would be NO JOY.
For there is a VERY big danger...as you try to reach
the top...that the furniture will come toppling down, and
would be VERY hard to stop.
Don't let an accident happen...because you want your toy
so much...for a bureau doesn't care who climbs
on it, or WHO it could instantly crush! (yikes!)
Be SMART and ask your parents...to give you a helping

hand...when you're reaching HIGH for that special toy,
they will surely understand.
Just remember, <u>DON'T</u> climb on furniture...for a toy
that you might see...for the furniture and ALL
could come toppling down...IT COULD BE
TOO <u>TOP-HEAVY</u>!

URGENT MESSAGE FROM MR. SEE-MORE SAFETY:

WARNING TO KIDS! Climbing on furniture can be extremely dangerous because it could suddenly get top-heavy as you begin climbing high and higher. It could fall straight down on YOU! The heavier the furniture is, the more dangerous it will be should it topple over. Never open drawers to help you climb because the furniture could fall forward. Don't <u>ever</u> pull items off of high shelves because it could cause heavier items to come crashing down. And <u>never</u> climb on boxes or other loose objects to try to reach the top. You could get injured. Be smart by "PLAYING IT SAFE!"

I FOUND A SHORT CUT

KIDS BE <u>AWARE</u> if you should happen to see...a POND
nearby that looks as TEMPTING as can be...
you should <u>NEVER</u> be fooled...by WHAT YOU SEE, cause
you could EASILY fall in and get hurt, BELIEVE ME!
It could be too deep. It could have thin ice. You just NEVER
know...so don't EVEN think twice!
You gotta do what's right. You gotta go the other way. You
gotta tell your friends...that you DON'T want to stay.
You gotta play it safe. You gotta do what's right. You gotta
lead your friends away...then you'll <u>ALL</u> BE ALL RIGHT!

URGENT MESSAGE FROM MR. SEE-MORE SAFETY:

Don't <u>EVER</u> go near a pond or body of water where there is no lifeguard. It may be enticing to show off or to try something different, just for the fun of it. Some kids are curious or tempted by new challenges and will take risks to prove how courageous they are. Maybe you believe that you are special and an accident can't happen to you. This is called "magical thinking" but it is not based on fact. Everyone is special, including YOU, but this does not change the fact that if a dangerous risk is present, an accident can happen sooner or later. "Playing it safe" by going the other way and refusing to take <u>ANY</u> chances will lead you in the right direction. You will have eliminated the risk of drowning in an ice covered pond. Remember, the smart choices you make <u>today</u> will help keep you safe <u>tomorrow</u>!

LAZY DAYS OF SUMMER

SWIMMING can be, oh, so much fun on a hot...summer day...
and these <u>VERY</u> important rules will help to KEEP IT...that way.
*Make SURE there is a lifeguard ALWAYS watching from the
chair. Don't <u>EVER</u> take a chance and swim if NO ONE...
is there.
*Before you dive into the pool...CHECK <u>FIRST</u>...TO SEE...how
deep the water <u>REALLY</u> is, FEET FIRST if it's at your knee.
*<u>NEVER</u> sit or play...near the drain of a swimming pool. Be sure
to keep your hair pinned back; please follow this lifesaving rule!
*<u>ALWAYS</u> have a buddy at a pool or at a lake...if you're there to
help each other...a FRIENDSHIP you will make!

35

By practicing these safe swimming tips, you will have, oh, so much fun...swimming at the neighborhood pool...under the midday sun.

URGENT MESSAGE FROM MR. SEE-MORE SAFETY:

KIDS, we all know how much fun swimming can be, but you must respect the danger of water. Don't allow yourself to become overconfident. You may feel you are a good swimmer and don't need to obey safety rules. This is the exact time you could get into serious trouble. Even Olympic swimmers know the importance of becoming extremely skilled in their area of strength and knowing where they need more practice before they can perform safely. So become a "SAFE SMART" swimmer, and help your buddy to become one too. After all, that's what buddies are for!

LEFT, RIGHT, AND LEFT AGAIN

CROSSING is as simple as one, two, three...if you will
learn these steps, you'll do just fine, YOU'LL SEE.
You must look left...right...and left again. You must
CHECK...FOR...CARS...around a bend. And when
you find...that...the time is right, you can SAFELY
cross to the other side.
But remember if...you...should...TALK to a FRIEND,
you must look left...right...and left again.
And when you see...that...there...are...NO CARS IN
SIGHT...you can SAFELY cross to the other side.

URGENT MESSAGE FROM MR. SEE-MORE SAFETY:

As you cross the street, continue to look left and right until you reach the other side. <u>NEVER</u> follow friends into the street without looking both ways yourself. Always check for cars turning from side streets. If you are trying to cross, and a car is parked to your left or right, inch out slowly until you get a clear view. Don't assume the coast is clear unless you know for sure. Make sure to double-check. Remember, crossing is a skill which requires very very good judgment. You must have the ability to determine how fast the cars in <u>ALL</u> lanes are coming, as well as their exact distance, in order to safely cross to other side. If there is a crosswalk, USE IT! It is much safer to cross when a traffic light is present because you can be seen more clearly. Practice with your parents until they say you have enough experience to cross alone.

THE MOTOR'S RUNNING

WARNING WARNING boys and girls, DON'T EVER
walk behind...a car whose motor's on or you might
SUDDENLY FIND...that the driver doesn't see you...
right behind his car...so ALWAYS move back kids,
move AWAY and move FAR!
You should NEVER walk between two cars as you
try to cross the street
The driver may not see you there and HEAD ON you
would meet.

A speeding car might whiz on by as if it's in a race...
and as you step into the road, you'd meet it FACE-TO-FACE.
Crossing between two cars...is <u>NOT</u> the way to go...
if you cross the right way EVERY TIME and DO IT RIGHT,
YOU'LL KNOW!
By taking these simple steps you'll be as SAFE AS YOU
CAN BE. By doing what is right, YOU WILL <u>PREVENT</u>
A TRAGEDY!!

URGENT MESSAGE FROM MR. SEE-MORE SAFETY:

Don't put yourself at risk by standing in-between two cars. A driver may not see you and begin backing up. There is also the danger of a gear slipping. If this occurs the car could suddenly roll back, pinning you. This could cause severe injury, or even be fatal. <u>NEVER</u> walk behind a vehicle when the motor is running unless the driver sees you and gives you the okay.

OFF TO SCHOOL

When you're getting on...or off the bus...it doesn't have
to be...a real big fuss...
You need to stand WAY back when the bus appears...
and wait PATIENTLY...as the bus nears.
And when the bus...stops...all you have to do...is climb up
the steps; I think you already knew.
And at the end of the day...when it's time to go home...
you need to exit the bus...as it has been shown.

"But Mr. See-More, notebook papers...just flew up in the air!" *"Don't <u>EVER</u> chase after them! Do you hear me? Don't you dare! The driver may not see you... underneath the wheel. If he should start to drive (Screeech!), you could get hit...FOR <u>REAL</u>!!"*

So step FAR AWAY until the coast is clear...and then you can cross...without any fear.
You need to <u>ALWAYS</u> DOUBLE CHECK that the coast is clear...and then you can cross...without ANY FEAR!

URGENT MESSAGE FROM MR. SEE-MORE SAFETY:

Always listen to the bus driver's instructions. Remember to stand 5 giant steps away from the bus as it approaches. <u>NEVER</u> run back for any items that drop in the street. Ask an adult to safely get the items for you!

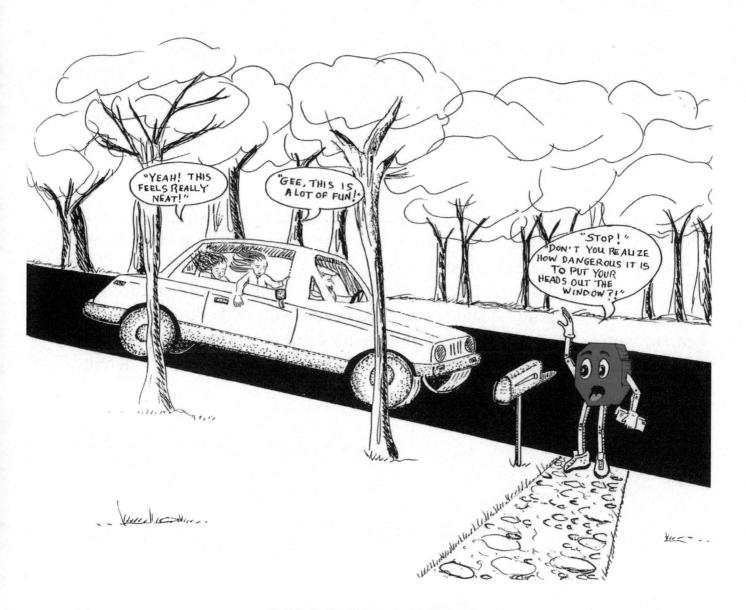

OUT FOR A RIDE

BOYS...AND...GIRLS...when you're IN A CAR...
keep your hands and your head in, you'll be
safer, BY FAR!
If you play with the windows...you may FAIL TO
SEE...that someone could get hurt...
VERY SERIOUSLY.
Keep them SAFE from harm. Keep them IN to stay.
You should NEVER put your hands...or your
head out to play.
So remember, HANDS and HEADS...DON'T
BELONG...OUTSIDE.

43

You've got to <u>PLAY</u>...<u>IT</u>...<u>SAFE</u>...when you're
OUT FOR A RIDE!

URGENT MESSAGE FROM MR. SEE-MORE SAFETY:

Children, do <u>NOT</u> play near or around power windows. If someone happens to put his hand or head in the path of a closing window, it could be extremely dangerous because most power windows have a lot of force and will not stop. Please understand that putting your head out of a window while a car is in motion is very unsafe. A sudden turn may cause you to be thrown out of the car, or worse, you could smack right into a tree or pole! This could be tragic. So "PLAY IT SAFE" and keep your ENTIRE body inside the car where it belongs.

OUT IN THE YARD

When you're out in the yard...you
should <u>NEVER</u> play...with dangerous
equipment...you should STAY AWAY.
There are hazards in the tool
shed...and the garage too...so <u>please</u>
don't go in...promise me, won't you?
This is <u>NOT</u> the place...for children
to be...they could get BADLY hurt
UNINTENTIONALLY! So when you

go out to play...learn to stay out
of harm's way...and your yard will be
a fun place each and every day.

BELOW is the ticket that was issued by See-More Safety's Yard Patrol:

1. A child was playing too close to the lawn mower. <u>Correction</u>: To prevent accidental injury, never play near lawn mowers while they are in operation.

2. A child was running under a garage door while it was closing. <u>Correction</u>: Never duck under a garage door as it is closing because someone could get trapped underneath and be crushed. The newest safety feature may still not reverse quickly enough in an emergency. PLAY IT SAFE! Always wait until the garage door is completely open – never closing – before going through.

3. Children were about to play with hazardous materials they found in a shed. <u>Correction</u>: Never play in or near sheds or garages where dangerous items, such as sharp electrical equipment, chemicals and flammable liquids, are stored. If they are used incorrectly, these products could be fatal!

On this day forward, the undersigned hereby promise to obey the rules of rules of the National Keep Our Yards Safe Campaign.

Date: _____

Signature of Offenders:_____

SAILING THE DEEP BLUE SEA

AHOY MATEYS, WELCOME ABOARD as you
sail the deep blue sea.
Make sure you have your life jacket on...and
would you save one for me?
For you NEVER know when a wave might arrive...
UNEXPECTEDLY!
And you'd be knocked right out of the boat thinking
"How could this happen to me?"
So please be prepared...AT ALL TIMES...for ANY
EMERGENCY.
As long as you have your life jacket on you will

47

HANDLE what will be...
when you're out on a boat trying to stay afloat,
while sailing the deep blue sea.

URGENT MESSAGE FROM MR. SEE-MORE SAFETY:

Please remember that wearing your life jacket could help save your life if you
ever fell overboard. Being prepared by having your life jacket on AT ALL
TIMES is your most important protection against an unexpected emergency.
Remember, no one can predict all possible dangers on the water. Even the
best swimmer cannot compete against a raging sea. Thinking ahead, by taking
all of the necessary precautions, is the key to being a responsible passenger.
So always be prepared!

SCHOOL DAYS

If you happen to be playing on the playground
at school...DON'T...TAKE...CHANCES...
BE EXTRA CAREFUL!
When you're climbing up...on the jungle gym...
it's okay to reach high...even up to your chin.
But DON'T EVER...HANG...A ROPE and do
tricks...cause you could get hurt BADLY,
ropes are NOT meant for this.
And NEVER...RUN AND CARRY...STICKS,

cause the TWO don't go together, they
don't <u>EVER</u> mix!
So remember, DON'T TAKE CHANCES...BE
<u>EXTRA</u> CAREFUL...when you're playing on
the playground at your neighborhood school.

URGENT MESSAGE FROM MR. SEE-MORE SAFETY:

When you are on the playground or in the yard, <u>NEVER</u> point or throw sharp objects, such as sticks, pencils, or swords at anyone. A child could suddenly trip and stab himself or someone else. There is also the possibility that a pointed object could hit someone directly in the eye, causing permanent injury. Be sure <u>NEVER</u> to hang ropes from trees, bunk beds, patio decks or other high areas. If you play with ropes inappropriately, they can be extremely dangerous wherever they happen to be.

A SPOONFUL OF CAUTION

WARNING to all kids who are home with the flu...if you
need to take medicine you should KNOW WHAT TO DO!
DON'T <u>EVER</u> take medicine when you're home for the day...
unless you are sure your mom says it's okay.
The very first step which is vital to see...is the medicine
you're taking and the prescription AGREE.
ALWAYS be sure that the dosage you take...is the exact
amount for your SIZE, AGE and WEIGHT.
As you put the teaspoon in your mouth TO BEGIN...please
DOUBLE-CHECK before LETTING IT IN!
NEVER take medicine if it's NOT meant for you...if you take

the wrong kind you could get SICKER, IT'S TRUE!
As you follow these tips you'll be SAFER, YOU'LL SEE...
and the medicine will help you AS FAST AS CAN BE!

URGENT MESSAGE FROM MR. SEE-MORE SAFETY:

Kids, you should <u>NEVER</u> take over-the-counter medication without help from your parents. It could be the wrong kind for your illness, or you could be allergic. The dosage may be too strong for your age and weight. It may not mix safely with a medicine you took that morning. If you happen to find medicine in a cabinet, it could be old and past the expiration date. If you were given permission to take over-the-counter medication after all safety measures have been taken, always leave it in its original container. Once you take the prescribed dosage, be <u>SURE</u> to put it out of the reach of your younger brothers and sisters.

THANKS FOR THE RIDE

When you're IN...A...CAR...and it's time to get out...there
are precautions to take...so you MUST...WATCH OUT!
You should <u>first</u>...make sure...right <u>before</u>...you go...that the
car comes to a stop, or it could ride on your toe. (Ouch!)
Always check with the driver...to make sure...and see...if
it's time to get out...if you BOTH AGREE.
As you slam the door shut, you need to double-check...that
little fingers are not there...the thought makes me a wreck!
So remember check FIRST...with the driver so you'll know...
that you've got the okay...the OKAY TO GO!

53

URGENT MESSAGE FROM MR. SEE-MORE SAFETY:

When you are getting out of a car, always check to make sure it has come to a complete stop. <u>Never</u> assume the driver understands what your intentions are. Instead, ask if it's okay to go, or wait until you get a sign such as a nod of the head indicating that the car has stopped and it is now all right for you to begin opening the car door. The main point is to be very clear when you are communicating with the driver so there are no misunderstandings, which could allow you to get hurt. Remember, always wait until the car has come to a complete stop before getting out, even if you are in a hurry! It is dangerous if the car is still in motion. Always make sure to get an okay from the driver before exiting the car to <u>guarantee</u> there are no misunderstandings.

THE NICE MAN

Don't talk to a stranger...because you NEVER KNOW...
who this stranger is...or the things that he might show...
to try to make you like him...in very sneaky ways.
Have you seen my dog? Here's some candy.
This is how he preys.
Kids be very cautious when you first meet someone new...
for you cannot always tell if this person is true blue.
So stay away from strangers...whoever they may be...
don't ever trust your faith in their CRED-I-BIL-I-TY.
Have your parents check to see who they <u>REALLY</u> are...

and you will be a SAFE SMART KID which will surely
take you far.

URGENT MESSAGE FROM MR. SEE-MORE SAFETY:

Did you know that a stranger is anyone you do not know? If a stranger comes up to you and asks you questions, be on the alert. Never put your name on the outside of your backpack or coat. This is where he may learn your name and pretend that he knows you when he really doesn't. No adult should be asking a child for directions, or help of any kind. This is a warning to STAY AWAY and to find a parent. If a car approaches you, cross to the other side and run in the opposite direction so you have time to get away. You have permission to scream as loud as you can. Never walk up to a car where the person could grab you. If you don't know this person, don't trust anything he says. It is better to be safe than sorry! Be a "SAFE SMART KID" by knowing what to do if a stranger approaches YOU!

THESE SHOES ARE MADE FOR WALKING

As you're walking home with friends...you can CLEARLY see...
that strolling in the street...is as DANGEROUS as can be.
Cars may JUST NOT see you as you're turning round a bend...
and by surprise you'd get hit by the driver's...FRONT END.
You <u>CANNOT</u> depend...on a motorist to see...your friends
and you WALKING where you SHOULDN'T BE.
Always face the traffic in a SINGLE FILE...as soon as there's
a sidewalk you can THEN WALK A MILE!
Make sure to wear reflectors...as day turns into night...for you
will NOT be seen if there is very little light.
Try to walk in groups for you'll be spotted EASILY...a child

walking by herself may be DIFFICULT TO SEE.
You can make the BEST and SAFEST choice when walking
home with friends. Stay off the streets—choose sidewalks—
THEY WILL HELP YOU IN THE END!

URGENT MESSAGE FROM MR. SEE-MORE SAFETY:

Boys and girls, walking in the street can be a serious danger, especially if you cannot be easily seen. Wherever possible, avoid walking in the street. This will eliminate the danger altogether! If there are no sidewalks, you need to reduce the risk to a minimum. You should always walk facing traffic. At night, carry a flashlight and wear retro-reflective clothing so you are visible to the driver. Reflective tape is also an excellent choice. It works just like bike reflectors and is available at fabric sporting goods, and hardware stores. If you are walking with a group, stay in a single file. There is a lot you can do to protect yourself by following all of the safety rules. Be a "safe smart kid" and remember to be extra careful when walking!

THINK BEFORE YOU ACT

BOYS AND GIRLS...it's important to see...that
making a sudden move...is as dangerous as can be.
If you happen to be out...on your bike for a ride...you
must check in <u>all</u> directions, then you go...in stride.
You should never act on impulse; don't act suddenly
you guys. You need to think WAY ahead...for
you may NOT get many tries!
You gotta THINK before you act. NEVER make a
sudden turn. ALWAYS check for danger first...
this is what you need to learn!

Remember: THINK before you act...NEVER make
a sudden turn...ALWAYS check for danger first...
THIS IS WHAT <u>YOU</u> NEED TO LEARN!

URGENT MESSAGE FROM MR. SEE-MORE SAFETY:

Adam made a good decision to get home quickly and off of his bike before the storm. The danger of lightning near trees or metal is a serious one because of the possibility of electrocution. But Adam went from one danger right into another when he decided to suddenly change directions. He acted impulsively as he turned the corner and came face to face with an oncoming car. He did not hesitate for the critical few seconds he needed to determine if it was safe for him to travel an unfamiliar route home. This could have turned out tragic if the driver wasn't able to slow down in time. So remember: <u>THINK</u> before you <u>ACT</u>, especially near the street!

THE TIE BREAKER

The PLAY-OFF game has finally begun, under the
sweltering heat of the hot summer sun.
As the game slowly goes from inning to inning...
it is my team I'm sure that's ahead and is winning.
As if out of nowhere...dark clouds appear...with a
THUNDERING ROAR that is following near.
The score is even, the tie breaker to begin...but
threatening lightning is moving in.
The coach blows his whistle and says "Stop the game!"
Spectators can be heard saying..."Oh, what a shame!"

A child screams out, "I see blue in the sky! Coach,
can't we give it just one more try?"
Another boy cries, "It's the end of the season, a little
lightning is not a good enough reason."
The coach bellows out, "This is a lesson to be learned!
It's never worth the chance of a person getting burned!
A baseball game can be played...ANYTIME, but risking a
life would be a SERIOUS CRIME.
Sooner or later you'd run out of luck, and that's the exact
time that you could get struck!"
So don't take <u>ANY</u> chances when a storm comes your way,
for there's always tomorrow...a whole bright new day.

URGENT MESSAGE FROM SEE-MORE SAFETY:

Lightning is dangerous! Go off the field and stay away from trees, metal
objects, and water. Stay low. Lightning will strike the highest object first.
Get to shelter as quickly as you can!

TIS THE SEASON TO BE SAFE

As winter approaches and snow fills the air, the laughter
of children can be heard everywhere.
There are dreams of snowmen just waiting to be made,
out of sparkling snowflakes that have quietly laid.
But danger abounds for those who don't know,
the harshness of December's cold winter snow.
As children dash out in the air filled with glee, they
must never forget winter's ferocity.
The very first thing that children should do, is dress

with warm hats, boots and woolen gloves too.
Snow suits and layers of clothes should be worn, to
build the best snowman and have time to adorn.
As children take their sleds to the highest of hills,
they must learn to prevent any dangerous spills.
Large trees should never stand right in the way of
the path your sled takes, a high price you could pay.
As snowball fights always know how to begin, just
make sure the snow's soft and not firmly packed in.
One dangerous throw could hit hard in the face, and
the fun the day brought would in an instant erase.
As you play carefully there will be much fun in store,
and the joy the season brings will be yours
EVERMORE!

URGENT MESSAGE FROM SEE-MORE SAFETY:

Always check to see if there are any obstacles in your path before sledding. If a hill is facing the street, this is where your sled will go, so "PLAY IT SAFE" and look for another hill. Then have oodles and oodles of winter fun!!

WHAT A GREAT VIEW

Sitting on a windowsill is dangerous for you see...
one small PUSH on a window screen could suddenly
set it free. Out you'd go...SCREEN and ALL, down one story,
two stories, three..until you'd hit rock bottom,
something NO ONE wants to see!
Don't EVER lean on windows, they could suddenly
give way, too!
Make SURE to keep your distance when you're
looking at the view.
So PLAY IT SMART when viewing from high...

65

stand BACK from windows and screens...
and you'll be SO MUCH SAFER as you
REACH...FOR YOUR DREAMS!

URGENT MESSAGE FROM MR. SEE-MORE SAFETY:

A window screen may give you a false sense of security that you are protected from a fall when you really aren't. It may not have been installed correctly or is in need of repair. You should <u>NEVER</u> lean back or forward on a screen or window because either one could suddenly give way when you least expect it. If you are enjoying the view, you should continue, but DO NOT assume that a second story window or screen is sturdy enough to lean against. And please, don't <u>EVER</u> lean out of a window to call a friend or to reach for something because you believe you won't fall. Remember: You don't have to <u>FALL</u> for a false belief!

WHAT'S COOKING?

Boys and girls, it's important to see...that the cooking area is NOT the PLACE
TO BE!
There are many hidden dangers...if you don't watch out...that could hurt
you VERY BADLY...that's WITHOUT A DOUBT!
You should <u>NEVER</u> play near burners...or reach for anything high...and
don't <u>EVER</u> wear loose clothing
that could catch a spark OH, MY!
ALWAYS turn pot handles in...so no one knocks them down. The liquid
that is boiling could come SPLASHING to the ground.

Don't run when carrying forks or knives; they are sharp and dangerous, too. As you follow these important rules, you'll be safer, I GUARANTEE YOU!

URGENT MESSAGE FROM MR. SEE-MORE SAFETY:

There are risks in the kitchen that can easily be avoided following the safety rules. <u>NEVER</u> run when carrying forks or knives. Carry sharp utensils by the handle and to your side, with the pointed end facing down. Don't hold food in the palm of your hand and then use a knife. It could slip and cut you. Did you know that nail polish remover is flammable? Flammable liquids should <u>NEVER</u> be kept above a stove or near a heat source. A drop of liquid could accidentally spill onto the burner causing an explosion and possible fire. You could get SERIOUSLY burned. Although the stove may be turned off, the flammable liquid — or the vapor surrounding it — could come in contact with the pilot light underneath. This may be an uncommon danger but when least expected, a scenario could develop which could lead to tragic consequences unless you know how to prevent it. So read labels <u>carefully</u> and store all flammable liquids away from the kitchen area.

WHAT'S IN THERE?

NEVER reach in places that you're not sure about...
for you just might find something sharp...
and you'd begin to shout!
"OUCH," what just cut me...inside that old bag?
All I thought was there...was a DIRTY OLD RAG!"
Never PUT a SPOON...or a FORK...or a KNIFE...
in <u>ANY</u> electrical appliance...it could cost you your
LIFE!
So NEVER reach in places that you're NOT sure about...
by being EXTRA cautious you'll be SAFER...
NO DOUBT!

URGENT MESSAGE FROM MR. SEE-MORE SAFETY:

<u>NEVER</u> put metal objects – or fingers – inside an electrical outlet, or socket. You could get electrocuted! Even after you disconnect the cord there may still be an electrical charge present, so "play it safe" when you're using appliances and ask an adult to help you if something isn't working properly. Sometimes children are curious and may act without thinking. For example, a child may reach his head into a small space to see what's inside and get stuck. If he can't get unstuck, he could suffocate! Reaching your arm into an unknown area may also be dangerous. Broken glass, sharp blades, or live electrical wires could be waiting on the other side. If you are curious, be sure what you're getting into. Be smart, and <u>NEVER</u> reach into places that you're <u>NOT</u> sure about!

YOU'RE A CHICKEN

You should NEVER...DARE...A FRIEND TO DO...
something that you know is wrong and dangerous, too.
DON'T play risky games...to prove who is best...
DON'T EVER put your friends to a dangerous test.
You'll be a TRUE friend...if you choose NOT to give a
dare...that could get your friends hurt...something you
COULDN'T REPAIR.
So NEVER...DARE...A FRIEND TO DO...something
that you KNOW is wrong and DANGEROUS, TOO!

71

URGENT MESSAGE FROM MR. SEE-MORE SAFETY:

It is important to understand that you may not mean any harm when you dare someone, but if it is a risky act, it could end up with tragic consequences. What may have begun as innocent fun may suddenly turn out to be dangerous, or even deadly. You need to think VERY seriously about putting anyone in a position where he has to choose between doing something on a dare, or else be laughed at by his peers. Most kids will do <u>ANYTHING</u> to be accepted by their friends, even if that means taking dangerous chances or doing risky things to prove their allegiance and bravery. They may feel this is the only way to be included in the group, but they may also be unaware of the true danger involved. If someone got seriously hurt as a result of a dare that you gave – even if it was unintentional – you would feel extremely remorseful. So remember: Be a TRUE FRIEND and DON'T... GIVE...DARES!

CALLING ALL KIDS

I would love to know the safe choices you are making. If you've been a "safe smart kid" by staying away from situations that are dangerous — or if you have chosen not to go along with your friends because they are taking unnecessary chances — please email me and you will receive a personal letter of recognition for "playing it safe" and for helping to lead the way to a safer world.

In the near future, I will be starting a "Play It Safe Kids Club." I will also have a newsletter entitled "Safe Smart Kids." I would like to include your positive stories in my newsletter in order to help other kids just like you. If you would like your story to be published, please let your mom or dad give permission in an email. Also state whether you would like your name and state to be mentioned. I cannot publish all of your letters, but there is a chance that yours may be chosen if it relates to the topic being discussed. It may one day be your story that influences a child to "PLAY IT SAFE."

Please send your success stories to: www.see-more-safety.com

I hope that all of my friends continue to help me with my job of keeping everyone safe and sound. I cannot do it without YOU!

Your friend,

Mr. See-More Safety™

GLOSSARY

accident - an unintended occurrence that results in loss, damage, or death. The <u>accident</u> occurred when she leaned over the balcony.

accidental - unexpected or unplanned. Although the drowning was <u>accidental</u>, the girl in charge felt terribly responsible.

acting on impulse - acting suddenly without any previous thought, delay, or caution. He was <u>acting on impulse</u> when he ran out into the street to catch the bus.

assume; assumption - to believe something but without proof. Don't <u>assume</u> Michael is picking you up unless you know for sure.

boomerang - to come back or return. If you pull on an object it may <u>boomerang</u>, causing a sharp ting as it snaps back.

careful - caution in one's actions; guarding against mistakes. In order to prevent a car accident, you must be extremely <u>careful</u> to stay alert at all times.

careless - not paying enough attention to what one does; having no care or concern. The teenager's <u>careless</u> actions caused the tragic accident at the intersection.

cause and effect - an event that produces a particular outcome as a direct result of the conditions preceding it. It is important to know the <u>cause and effect</u> of certain actions so you will know how to avoid them.

caution - concern for safety; unwillingness to take chances. The boy used extreme <u>caution</u> as he began working with the sharp tools.

chance - a possibility of something happening. We made sure there was no <u>chance</u> for the children to find the medicine.

chicken - (1a) A negative term meaning coward, used by a bully to get
someone to do something risky. (1b) A dangerous game that challenges
someone to do. Playing <u>chicken</u> while driving caused the boy to get
killed.

consequences - the result of something that happened earlier. If you are
careless by leaving matches where small children are playing, there
could be tragic <u>consequences</u>.

critical - of extreme importance at a time of danger. The <u>critical</u> few seconds
it takes to hesitate before running into the street could be the difference
between life and death.

crosswalk - an area marked with painted lines that is used by pedestrians to
help them safely cross the street. Always use a <u>crosswalk</u> to help you
across a busy street.

curious - the desire to learn or to know about anything. An was so <u>curious</u>,
she went in the cave and then couldn't find her way out.

dangerous - very unsafe, open to harm or injury. It is very <u>dangerous</u> for
children to be walking where there is no sidewalk.

dare - to challenge a person to do something risky. It is wrong to <u>dare</u>
someone to do anything that could cause physical harm.

dart - to suddenly begin running without looking. As Amy began to <u>dart</u> into
the street to catch her pet rabbit, she almost got hit by a car.

defensive - used or intended to defend or protect. Become a <u>defensive</u> driver,
and learn to watch out for the other guy.

distract - putting one's attention on something less important than the present
situation. If you <u>distract</u> me while driving, I won't be able to
concentrate.

dosage - an amount of medicine to be taken at one time. The correct <u>dosage</u> should be given according to the child's age and weight.

double-check - to check twice or recheck to make sure a situation is safe. Justin had to <u>double-check</u> to make sure the stove was turned off.

electrocution - causing death due to the passage of a high voltage of electricity through the body. Touching inside of an appliance with damp hands can cause <u>electrocution</u>.

emergency - a sudden need for immediate action What began as a small fire suddenly turned into an <u>emergency</u> as the flames quickly spread through the house.

expiration date - the date on the label that tells you when a medicine should be thrown away because it is no longer safe or effective. The girl noticed that the medicine was past the <u>expiration</u> date and had to call her doctor for a new prescription.

false belief - a belief that something is true when it is based on mistaken facts or false ideas. She had the <u>false belief</u> that nothing would happen to her even though she was driving much too fast for the weather conditions.

flammable - easily set on fire; combustible. It is important to read the warning on the label to make sure the liquid is not <u>flammable</u>.

hazardous - dangerous, risky. Driving during the thunderstorm was very <u>hazardous</u> because of the possibility of flash flooding.

Heimlich maneuver - an emergency procedure to help a person that is choking by an upper abdominal thrust that forces air from the lungs upward to dislodge the obstruction. Learning the <u>Heimlich maneuver</u> could help save someone's life.

hesitate - to be reluctant or wait to act. She remembered to <u>hesitate</u> before running after her dog who had darted into the street.

high tension wires - overhead wires that bring electricity to the neighborhood which contain an extremely high voltage of electricity. Never play with kites near <u>high tension wires</u> because of the danger of electrocution.

impulsive - acting suddenly, without forethought. Running into the street without checking first is an <u>impulsive</u> move.

lifeline - assistance at a critical time. The rope that was thrown to the man in the burning building was his only <u>lifeline</u>.

lightning - the bright flashes of electricity in the sky that usually occur during a thunderstorm. <u>Lightning</u> carries a high voltage of electricity so stay inside during thunderstorms.

magical thinking - thinking that is not supported by fact. <u>Magical thinking</u> is dangerous for it could lead you to make unsafe choices.

misunderstanding - failure to understand the meaning of a person's statement, causing possible confusion. A <u>misunderstanding</u> can be tragic when you are watching small children at a swimming pool.

noose - a loop that has a knot which tightens as it is pulled. A simple loop made out of rope could become a dangerous <u>noose</u> if you put it around your neck.

overconfident - too confident or sure of yourself. This attitude could result in an accident because you may become careless the more <u>overconfident</u> you become. Marc became overconfident and cut himself with a knife as he began working too fast.

pedestrian - a person who goes or travels on foot; walker. In high traffic areas, it is important for the <u>pedestrian</u> to cross only when the crosswalk signal gives the go ahead.

pilot light - a small light that is kept burning all the time and is used to turn on a main light whenever needed. If a pilot light goes out, the dial on the gas stove should be turned off for a few minutes before relighting it.

possibility - something that can happen or occur. By taking the proper precautions, the possibility of an accident is much less likely.

precaution - an action taken beforehand to prevent an unwanted situation from occurring; forethought. Judy took every precaution to avoid getting bitten by the snake.

prescription - a doctor's written directions on the use of a specific medicine. The medicine you need requires a doctor's prescription.

prevention - to keep from occurring. The prevention of accidents can be accomplished with knowledge desire, and effort.

prey - an object or victim of attack. Ships often become the prey of pirates.

risk - the possibility of injury or loss; a hazard or dangerous chance. You can avoid the risk of injury by being extra careful.

safeguard - a protection or defense that ensures safety. Wearing your seatbelt is the best safeguard against an unexpected accident.

scenario - the circumstances leading up to an accident. Observing a dangerous scenario in advance will help identify hidden risks.

suffocation - preventing air to the blood through the lungs causing death. Getting trapped in a small, enclosed space can cause suffocation.

toggles – a pin, rod, or crosspiece fitted or inserted into a loop in a rope, chain, or strap to prevent slipping, to tighten, or to hold an attached object. It is important to remove all toggles from scarves and drawstrings before going to the playground.

top-heavy - much heavier above the center. As the top drawers opened, the filing cabinet became top-heavy and began to fall over.

tragedy - a very sad or terrible happening, often resulting in severe injury or death. We can prevent tragedy by eliminating risky behaviors.

uninsulated - an electrical wire that is not protected by a covering. Never touch wires that have fallen because they are uninsulated.

unintentional - not done on purpose or with the desire to cause harm. Although it was unintentional, Jill's carelessness caused the baby's near drowning and the need to be rushed to the nearest hospital.

vapor - a highly flammable gas formed from a liquid or solid chemical. The invisible vapor could cause a dangerous explosion.

visibility - the state of being able to see or be seen. Because of the snow storm, our visibility was almost zero.

voltage - the strength of electrical force running through a wire. Overhead electrical wires contain a high voltage of electricity.

DON'T MISS OUT ON MORE OF MR. SEE-MORE SAFETY'S
BOOKS AND PRODUCTS.

IF YOU AND YOUR KIDS ENJOYED THIS BOOK, WOULD YOU
KINDLY TAKE A MOMENT TO GIVE ME A 5 STAR REVIEW?
YOUR ENDORSEMENT WILL GREATLY HELP ME IN MY EFFORT
TO SPREAD MY SAFETY MESSAGE NEAR AND FAR.

BE SURE TO BOOKMARK THIS WEBSITE SO YOU CAN BE
UPDATED ON EXCITING EDUCATIONAL MATERIALS COMING
SOON! THESE BOOKS AND PRODUCTS ARE DESIGNED TO GIVE
YOUR CHILD THE BEST SAFETY EDUCATION POSSIBLE!

www.see-more-safety.com

MAY YOU AND YOUR LOVED ONES ALWAYS BE SAFE AND
SOUND!

ABOUT THE AUTHOR

Janis Rafael is a graduate of the University of Maryland and holds a Bachelor of Science degree in special education. She has done extensive research on safety and has developed a comprehensive program to help children have a better understanding of the nature of risk, and what it means to be careful. From her research she has discovered there is a gap in knowledge between the ages of 5 and 11 years old. Children are taught to use their helmets and call 911 in an emergency but have very little training on how to identify serious dangers in their environment, or what they can do to avoid them. Her program is aimed at filling that gap. This proactive approach also emphasizes assertiveness training to encourage children to find answers to questions they may need before starting a new activity. Her goal is to help them distinguish between risks that are worth taking and those that have the potential for tragedy. She believes that the more information we share with our youth, the safer our society will be since they will be basing their decisions on genuine understanding. In her opinion it isn't knowledge that can harm our youth, it is the lack of it. We cannot afford leaving to chance crucial safety information that our children must have in order to make informed choices. The price may be far too high.

Discussions regarding responsibility are an integral part of her program. This is a necessary ingredient because it allows children to have a greater understanding of the consequences of their behavior. Without these discussions they may think only in terms of the legal repercussions without considering the hurt to innocent bystanders that could result. They need to recognize the importance of being as careful as possible in situations where their actions could have a direct impact on others. Unfortunately, young people often think only in terms of whether there is a risk to themselves. She hopes to address this issue as well as other contributing factors that may lead children down a negative path of irresponsibility.

Ms. Rafael has four children and fourteen grandchildren. She resides in Palm Beach, Florida.

Made in the USA
Columbia, SC
13 October 2022

69270744R00050